STORM
IS COMING!

by **Heather Tekavec**
illustrated by **Margaret Spengler**

Dial Books for Young Readers **New York**

For Tatiana and Catherine
—H.T.

To my husband, Ken Spengler, my biggest supporter
—M.S.

Published by Dial Books for Young Readers
A division of Penguin Putnam Inc.
345 Hudson Street
New York, New York 10014
Text copyright © 2002 by Heather Tekavec
Illustrations copyright © 2002 by Margaret Spengler
All rights reserved
Designed by Kimi Weart
Text set in Beton
Printed in Hong Kong on acid-free paper

10 9 8 7 6 5 4 3 2 1

Library of Congress Cataloging-in-Publication Data
Tekavec, Heather, date.
Storm is coming! / by Heather Tekavec;
illustrated by Margaret Spengler.
p. cm.
Summary: The animals misunderstand the farmer's
"Storm" warning and expect someone scary and mean.
ISBN 0-8037-2626-0
[1 Storms—Fiction. 2. Domestic animals—Fiction.]
I. Spengler, Margaret, ill. II. Title.
PZ7.T2345 St 2002
[E]—dc21   00-034622

The art was created using pastels.

The old farmer leaped out of his chair and clicked the radio off.

"Hear that, Dog?" he bellowed. "Storm is coming! We better get the animals safely in the barn!"

Dog sprang to his feet and bounded out the door.
"Round 'em up!" the farmer called as Dog ran circles around the sheep.

"Storm is coming! Storm is coming!" barked Dog. "We have
to get to the barn quickly!"
Frightened, the sheep raced after Dog toward the barn.

On the way, they passed the pond where Duck was paddling.

"Sto-o-orm is coming! Sto-o-orm is coming!" the sheep bleated.

"We have to get to the ba-a-arn quickly!"

Duck flapped up the grassy bank and flew ahead of the sheep.

The cows in the pasture looked up as the animals sped past.

"Storm is coming! Storm is coming!" Duck quacked. "We have to get to the barn quickly!"

The cows herded together and joined the stampede. When they all reached the barn, the farmer hurried them inside. Then he shut the heavy door.

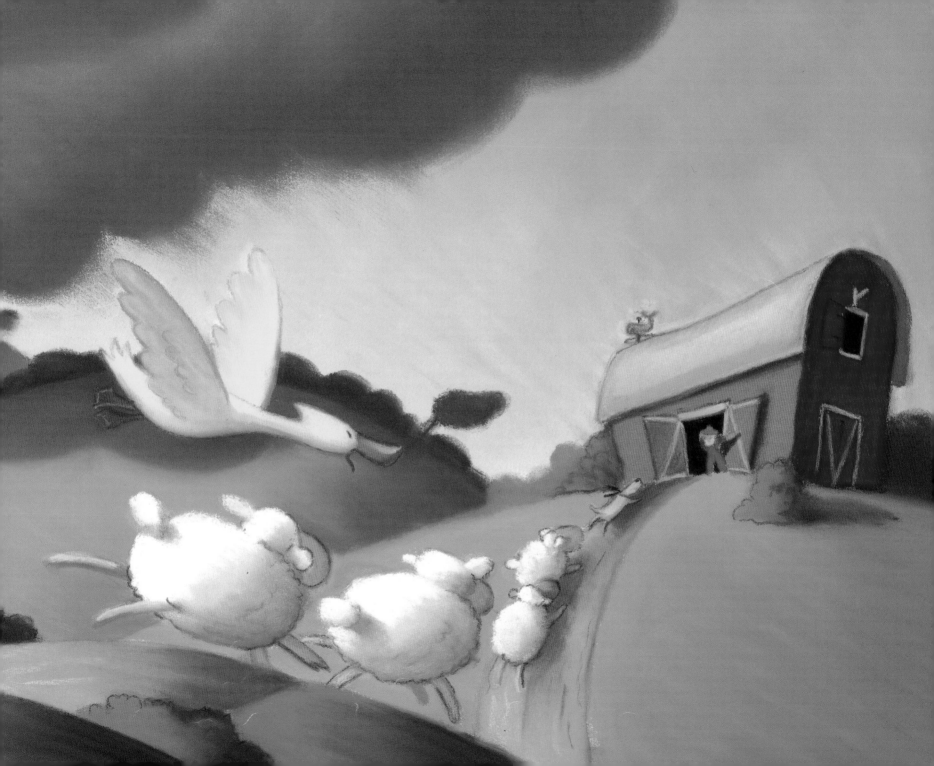

The barking, the flapping, the bleating, and the mooing awoke
Cat from her nap in the hay. She stretched and yawned and
opened one eye.

"STORM IS COMING!" the animals told her all at once.

"And who is Storm?" she meowed.

The cows looked at Duck.
Duck looked at the sheep.
The sheep looked at Dog.
But Dog didn't know.

"Well, he must be very mean," Dog decided, moving to guard the door.

"And he must be-e-e very sca-a-a-ry!" the sheep stammered, starting to shiver.

"Big . . . Big . . . He must be very big!" Duck sputtered,
flapping into the air in a flurry.

The cows just lay in the corner and moaned.

Cat yawned again. "Wake me when he gets here,"
she murmured, and drifted back to sleep.

The animals waited and listened,
but there was no sign of Storm.
   "We need a lookout!" Dog barked.
   Duck flew up to the open window
and cautiously peeked out.
   "No Storm. No Storm!" he quacked.
"But the sky is growing very dark."

"Oh no-o-o!" bleated the sheep. "Even the su-u-u-n is hiding from Sto-o-o-rm!"

The cows dropped their heads and moaned louder.

"Dark is good!" Dog told them. "Storm can't find us in the dark."

The animals nodded. "That *is* good," they agreed.

Duck called down again, "I still don't see Storm, but there's a big wind blowing."

"Great!" Dog barked. "The wind will blow Storm away."

The cows lifted their heads and the sheep stopped shaking.

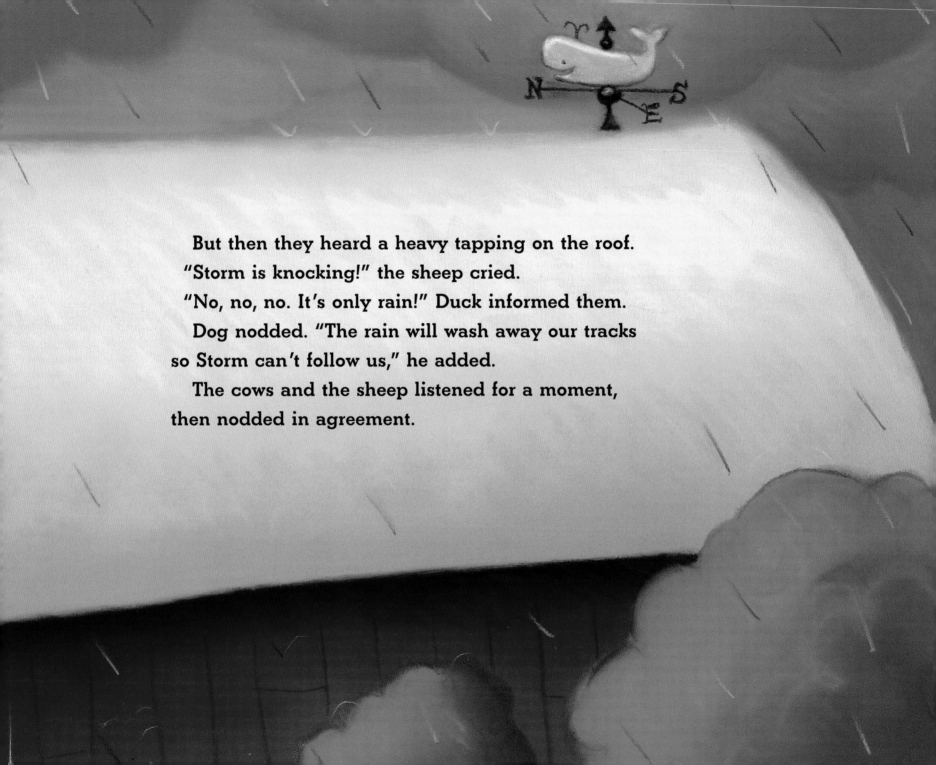

But then they heard a heavy tapping on the roof.

"Storm is knocking!" the sheep cried.

"No, no, no. It's only rain!" Duck informed them.

Dog nodded. "The rain will wash away our tracks so Storm can't follow us," he added.

The cows and the sheep listened for a moment, then nodded in agreement.

One more time, Duck called down, "I still don't see Storm, but the sky is flashing!"
"The sky is going to blind Storm so he can't see us!" Dog announced.
The cows scrambled to their feet and the sheep started shuffling.

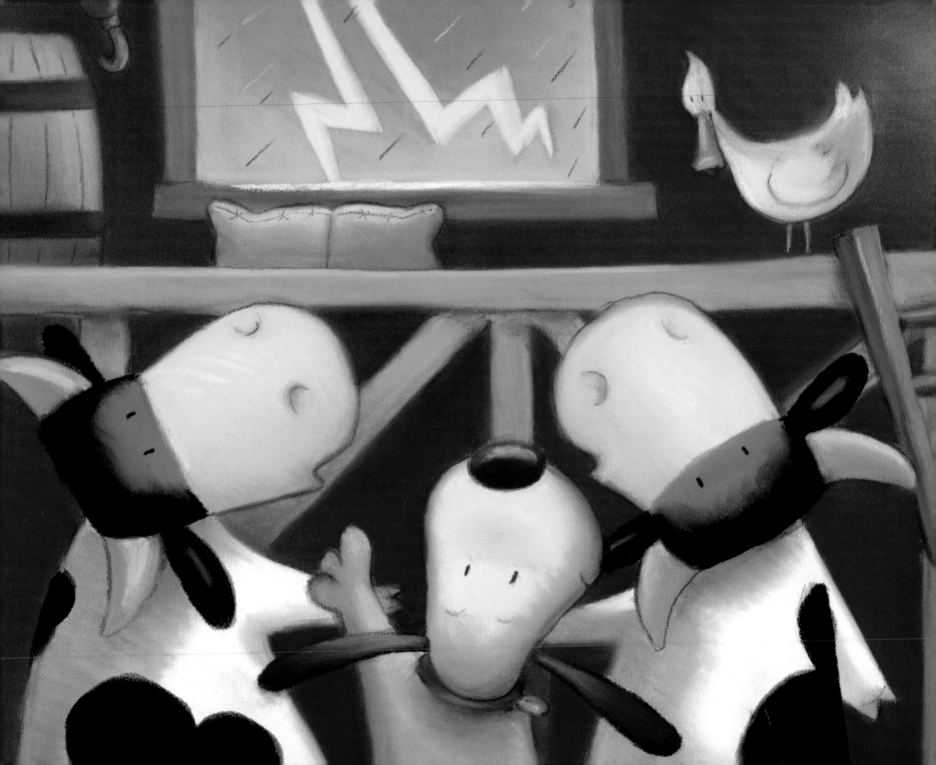

A roll of thunder shook the barn.

"Hear that, Duck?" Dog barked.

"Yes! Yes!" Duck quacked. "The clouds are growling at Storm. They'll scare him away for sure!"

All day long, the wind blew, the rain fell, the lightning flashed, and the thunder rolled. And through it all, the animals cheered.

But then everything stopped.

The sky went silent and so did the animals.
They waited and listened,
and Duck flew down to huddle with the others.

Thump, thump, thump. Someone was coming toward the barn.
Click, click, clang. Someone was opening the door.
Cre-e-e-eak. . . . Someone was coming in!
The animals backed into the corner. This was it. Storm had come
to get them!
The door swung wide open and the animals gasped. . . .

Thump, thump, thump. Someone was coming toward the barn.
Click, click, clang. Someone was opening the door.
Cre-e-e-eak. . . . Someone was coming in!
The animals backed into the corner. This was it. Storm had come
to get them!
The door swung wide open and the animals gasped. . . .

It was the farmer!
"Everybody out!" he called. "It's all safe now."
"Hurray!" shouted the animals.

The barking, the flapping, the bleating, and the mooing awoke Cat again. She stretched and yawned and opened one eye.

"Did I miss Storm?" she meowed.

"No," Dog reported. "Storm never came." Then he ran out into the sunshine with the others.

And Cat went back to sleep.